A HISTORICAL ALBUM OF
MASSACHUSETTS

A HISTORICAL ALBUM OF

MASSACHUSETTS

Monique Avakian

THE MILLBROOK PRESS, Brookfield, Connecticut

Front and back cover: "View of the City of Boston from Dorchester Heights."
Painted and engraved by Robert Havell, New York, 1840.
Courtesy of the New York Public Library.

Title page: View of Amherst College. Courtesy of Amherst College.

Library of Congress Cataloguing-in-Publication Data

Avakian, Monique.
    A historical album of Massachusetts / Monique Avakian.
        p. cm. — (Historical albums)
    Includes bibliographical references and index.
    Summary: A history of Massachusetts, from pre-Colonial days
to the present, highlighting the state's economic and cultural
development.
    ISBN 1-56294-481-9 (lib. bdg.) ISBN 1-56294-762-1 (pbk.)
    1. Massachusetts—History—Juvenile literature. 2. Massachusetts—
Gazetteers—Juvenile literature. [1. Massachusetts—History]
I. Title. II. Series.
F64.3.A93 1994
974.4—dc20   93-39014
                                                      CIP
                                                        AC

 Created in association with Media Projects Incorporated

    C. Carter Smith, *Executive Editor*
    Lelia Wardwell, *Managing Editor*
    Monique Avakian, *Principal Writer*
    Bernard Schleifer, *Art Director*
    Shelley Latham, *Production Editor*
    Arlene Goldberg, *Cartographer*

    Consultant: Edward Lerner, Social Studies Coordinator, Newton
Public Schools, Newton, Massachusetts

Copyright © 1994 by The Millbrook Press, Inc.

Manufactured in the United States of America

10 9 8 7 6 5 4 3 2 1

CONTENTS

Introduction   6

Part I:
The Bay State   7

Part II:
Changing Times   31

A Massachusetts Gazetteer   54

Resource Guide   62

Index   63

Introduction

Throughout the history of America, Massachusetts has led the nation in reform, industry, and scientific achievement. Its story includes many American heroes. Squanto taught the Pilgrims how to survive. Paul Revere called the Minutemen to action. Crispus Attucks, a free black, was one of the first Americans to die in the Revolutionary War. Lucy Stone braved hostile crowds to speak of women's rights. And John F. Kennedy, grandson of a penniless Irish immigrant, inspired the nation to greatness.

Geography has shaped the state's growth as well. Although one of the smallest states in the nation, Massachusetts contains a wide variety of landscapes. The western half of the state includes parts of the Berkshire and Taconic mountain ranges. Moving eastward, these hills give way to a plateau and then the fertile Connecticut River Valley. The southeastern portion is a sandy plain, providing beaches and secure harbors all along the Atlantic Coast.

Boston's harbor was a natural boon to the English colonists who arrived in the 1600s. The community would grow into a great port city, attracting immigrants and industry from all over the world. Massachusetts's rivers powered the nation's first mills. Abundant fish have been a source of food and economic gain for centuries. Today both the state's famous heritage and its beautiful natural features attract visitors from all over.

Massachusetts has a remarkable history of American leaders, reform movements, and advances in both culture and science. These contributions carry on today, and are firmly in place to guide the state and its people into the future.

PART ONE

THE BAY STATE

During the 1700s and early 1800s, Nantucket, Cape Cod, and Martha's Vineyard all prospered from the whaling industry. Crews on whaling ships harpooned the whales at close range, as shown in this print by Currier and Ives.

Massachusetts experienced tremendous changes in the 200 years after the Europeans first arrived in the 1600s. The explorers and first colonists encountered Native American groups who had kept to the same way of life for centuries. The newcomers brought change instantly, clearing the forests for farming, building towns, establishing governments and leaders. The Bay State led America's struggle to gain independence from Britain. In the beginning of the 19th century Massachusetts helped usher in a new era of industry, as mills and factories appeared along its major rivers.

Native Life before the Europeans

Native Americans came to what is now New England more than 10,000 years ago. Tribes in the Massachusetts region included the Pennacooks, the Nausets, the Pocomtucs, the Massachusets, the Nipmucs, and the Wampanoags. All six tribes belong to the Algonquian language group. The Wampanoags have always played a key role in the state's history. Today, tribal members live on the island of Martha's Vineyard and in Mashpee, on Cape Cod. Other tribes, such as the Massachusets, have since disappeared.

The earliest Native Americans gathered food as they found it. They moved around constantly and followed the animals they hunted. As tribes became more settled, they learned how to grow crops. Farming led to a great change of life for the Wampanoags. Corn, beans, squash and pumpkins were the Wampanoags' most important crops.

The Wampanoags lived in small dome-shaped huts called wigwams. The women made wigwams by bending wooden poles and covering them with tree bark or woven mats. Each dwelling had a fire pit in the middle of the floor for cooking and warmth. Smoke from the fire escaped through a hole cut in the roof.

The Indians left their homes in the wintertime to track game such as bear, deer, rabbit, and wild turkey. Hunting tools included spears, arrows, clubs, and traps. Massachusetts's native residents found a use for almost every part of the animal they hunted. They made bones into sewing needles and fish hooks, bladders into bags, and tendons into thread. They made clothes and shoes out of deerskin.

Some food came from rivers and lakes and—for groups who lived on the coast—the ocean. The Algonquian Indians traveled swiftly in canoes to hunt, fish, and trade with other tribes. Men used harpoons, nets, and traps to catch fish. Fish and animal meat were dried over a smoking fire in a process that preserved the food for future use.

The village shaman, or medicine man, healed the sick with herbs and special ceremonies. The shaman had no power, however, to stop diseases brought to America by European explorers. Native Americans had never been exposed to diseases like smallpox and measles, so they had no natural defenses against these illnesses, which spread quickly. By 1618, outbreaks of smallpox and measles cut the Indian population in the Massachusetts region by almost two-thirds. The arrival of Europeans to the New World had changed the Native American way of life forever.

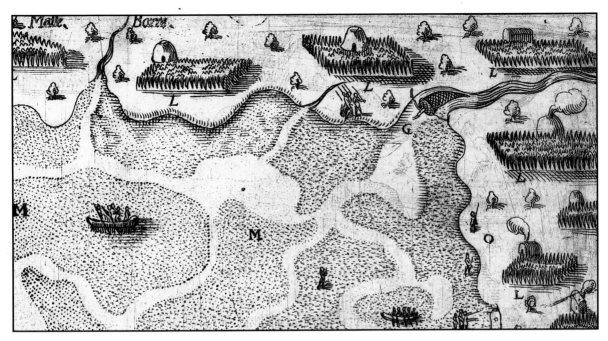

Coastal Native American tribes planted their cornfields right beside their wigwams, as shown in this 1605 engraving of Nauset Harbor (above). After the harvest, the Indians moved inland for the winter.

Corn (or maize) was first cultivated by the Native Americans. The Wampanoags of Massachusetts grew the crop to feed both the tribe and their livestock.

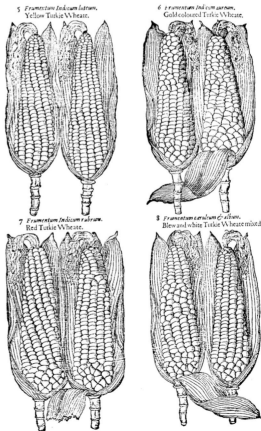

5 *Frumentum Indicum luteum.*
Yellow Turkie Wheate.

6 *Frumentum Indicum aureum.*
Gold coloured Turkie Wheate.

7 *Frumentum Indicum rubrum.*
Red Turkie Wheate.

8 *Frumentum cæruleum & albium.*
Blew and white Turkie Wheate mixed

Early Exploration

Many historians believe that the first Europeans to visit North America were the Vikings. Leif Ericson probably landed off the coast of Labrador sometime in the year 1000. Ericson may have sailed as far south as Chesapeake Bay. According to legend, he named the area where he landed Vinland, because he found so many grapes growing there. The Vikings may have tried to colonize this area (which some historians think included parts of what is now New England), but they did not stay for very long. Since they did not record their travels at that time, news of their discovery did not spread to Europe.

The next visitor from Europe reached North America in 1524. Giovanni da Verrazano, an Italian explorer who was employed by the French, sailed up the Atlantic Coast and discovered the New York and Narragansett bays. Some historians believe that Verrazano may have met two Wampanoag chiefs during the expedition. French explorer Samuel de Champlain also visited Massachusetts, in 1605 and 1606, while mapping the Atlantic Coast. The French left the region, however, choosing instead to settle territory in Canada and New York close to the St. Lawrence River.

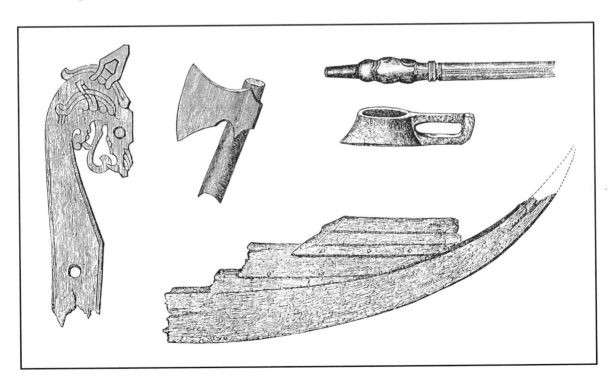

The first Europeans to live in Massachusetts stayed for only a short time. Englishman Bartholomew Gosnold arrived in the spring of 1602. He and his crew sailed along the Atlantic Coast from Maine to Rhode Island. Gosnold explored and named Cape Cod, Martha's Vineyard, and the Elizabeth Islands—including Cuttyhunk Island, where he built a house and a fort. Once settled, the explorers planted a garden and traded for furs with the Indians. These efforts were not enough to sustain the group, however, and eventually a shortage of supplies forced Gosnold to give up his plan for settlement. His group returned to England.

Gosnold made it back to America in 1607 with Captain John Standish

The Vikings are believed to have been the first European visitors to North America. This engraving (opposite) shows some artifacts of a Viking ship, including a dragon head prow (forward tip of a ship) and an ax.

In 1602, explorer Bartholomew Gosnold received gifts of cooked fish and tobacco from friendly Wampanoags when he landed on Cape Cod, as shown in this illustration (above). Stories of peaceful trade with the Indians encouraged other European explorers to come to New England.

and others. They founded America's first permanent colony in Jamestown, Virginia. Captain Smith went on to explore and map all of New England. In 1616, he published *A Description of New England*, a book that encouraged many Europeans to come to the New World.

The first Europeans to settle permanently in the Massachusetts area were actually trying to get to Virginia. This group of English men and women, now known as the Pilgrims, came to America so they could practice their religion freely. Their ship, called the *Mayflower*, set sail from England on September 6, 1620.

The voyage across the Atlantic Ocean was difficult. Illness and hunger were constant threats to the group. By the end of the journey, the only food available was salt horse (salted beef, pork, or fish) and hardtack (dry biscuits). After a while, water stored aboard was no longer safe to drink, so everyone, including the children, drank beer. The Pilgrims

When the Pilgrims reached Plymouth in 1620, winter had already set in. Most of the passengers remained on board ship, while the scouts and leaders set up a camp on the shore and went about choosing a site for settlement.

disapproved of the sailors' bad language, and the sailors made fun of the seasick Pilgrims, calling them "glib-gabbety puke stockings."

On November 9, 1620, a shout rang out from the ship's crow's nest: "Land-ho!" The Pilgrims, blown off course by storms, anchored at the site of Provincetown, on Cape Cod. On December 16 the Pilgrims founded their permanent home on the mainland, which became known as Plymouth Colony.

Pilgrims and Puritans

The Puritans, like the Pilgrims, did not want to worship God in the way the King of England said they should. The Pilgrims wanted to separate completely from the Church of England, while Puritans wanted to "purify" the church and change it from within to suit their religious views. King James I and King Charles I punished both groups for meeting secretly, which is why they came to America seeking religious freedom and economic opportunity.

The Pilgrims faced two pressures when they reached America. One was

Soon after settling, the Pilgrims planted vegetable gardens and built their houses with timber planks and thatched roofs. Their village exists today as a living museum, re-creating 17th-century daily life for visitors, as shown in this photograph.

to survive in the wilderness by providing food and shelter. The other was to find ways to pay back the people who had financed their journey. A group of London investors had given the Pilgrims money with the hope that great riches would be found in the New World. In addition to providing such supplies as food and tools, and paying for the voyage, the investors hired seventy seamen, craftsmen, and laborers to help the Pilgrims build their colony.

Samoset, a sachem (chief) of the Pemaquid tribe of Maine, was the first Native American the Pilgrims met. He surprised the settlers when he strolled into Plymouth and said, "Welcome, Englishmen." Samoset had learned English from European traders he had encountered earlier. He told the Pilgrims that their land belonged to the Patuxets, a Wampanoag sub-tribe. All but one Patuxet had died in the smallpox epidemic of 1616–17. The survivor's name was Squanto. Samoset brought Squanto to meet the Pilgrims a few days later.

Squanto taught the settlers how to hunt and fish more effectively. He showed them how to plant corn, using fish as fertilizer. Squanto also helped the Pilgrims negotiate a peace treaty with Wampanoag chief Massasoit on March 22, 1621. This pact, the first between Native Americans and European settlers, lasted for more than forty years.

Nearly half of the Pilgrims died during the brutal first winter of 1620. In the fall of 1621 the Pilgrims and about ninety Wampanoag Indians sat down for the first Thanksgiving feast. The hardest part was over, and soon the colony began to flourish, reaching a total population of 2,500 by 1640. The colony paid off its debt to its sponsors in 1648, mainly by shipping timber and beaver fur to England.

English settlers who came later to set up new colonies learned from the Pilgrims' mistakes. On March 29, 1630, when Captain John Winthrop and a group of about 1,000 Puritans left England, they were much better prepared for what lay ahead. They anchored in Salem, but went on to establish a number of different towns in the area. A group of about 150 Puritans lived on a hilly peninsula called Shawmut. Their village was officially named Boston on September 7, 1630. Two years later, Boston became the colony's capital.

John Winthrop was the first governor of the Massachusetts Bay Colony. He felt strongly that the colony should be a model for the rest of the world. The Puritans wanted to put their religion into practice and show the world that they had created a new society—"a visible kingdom of God."

Puritan minister John Cotton also played a key role in the government of the colony during this time. He and John Winthrop turned the Massachusetts Bay Colony into a church-run commonwealth. Sunday, for example, was the Lord's Day, when everyone had to go to church in the morning and again in the afternoon. No one was allowed to work or play. Since cooking on Sunday was considered a sin, women made Sunday's baked beans the night before. This common dish earned Boston the nickname Beantown.

Although Winthrop's Puritans left England to seek religious freedom, they denied that freedom to others. Quakers who came to preach in Boston were whipped in public, then expelled from the town. Banished Quakers who returned were subject to hanging. Many of those settlers who disagreed with the Puritans in their beliefs left Massachusetts and went on to establish other colonies in Rhode Island, Connecticut, New Hampshire, and Maine.

The Puritans placed a high value on education. They cared that their children were properly educated so that they could read the Bible. This keen emphasis on high-quality education led to the founding of the first schools in America. Boston Latin, opened in 1635, was America's first secondary school, and Harvard College, founded in Cambridge in 1636 to train future ministers, was the first college. America's first printing press, ironworks, and newspaper were also products of Puritan Massachusetts.

The Puritan clergy's power was not questioned until the hysteria of the Salem witchcraft trials broke out. The problems in Salem started in March

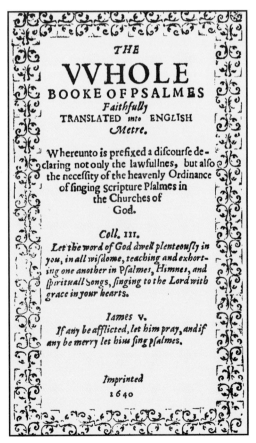

Quaker beliefs—that people have a direct link to God and don't need clergymen—threatened the power of the Puritan church in the Massachusetts Bay Colony. In this engraving (above, right), a Quaker preaches in a public square, an illegal activity.

Only eleven copies of the Bay Psalm Book (right) exist today. Stephen Daye printed the text in 1640 on a press located in a cow yard next to Harvard College. It was the first book to be published in North America.

Cotton Mather (above) was an important Puritan leader, both in church and government. He played a key role in the Salem witchcraft trials of 1692, but later questioned the proceedings. Mather also encouraged the use of the first smallpox vaccine.

During King Philip's War, the Indians often made successful surprise attacks against the colonists. In the end, however, the colonists won, mainly because of their superior weapons, as shown in this print (opposite) of a skirmish.

1692, when a group of young girls began to behave strangely. The people concluded that the girls were bewitched. Puritan minister Cotton Mather strengthened the townspeople's fear by preaching about the evils of witchcraft. By September 22, nineteen people had been hanged and twenty-seven had been convicted. Even two dogs were tried as witches and killed. Only when the governor's wife and other leading citizens were accused did the court begin to question the evidence that was gathered against the defendants.

Meanwhile, tensions between colonists and the Native Americans were increasing. In 1643, the Massachusetts Bay, Plymouth, Connecticut, and New Haven colonies formed the New England Confederation to unite in their defense against Indian attacks. Wampanoag leader King Philip did not cooperate with the colonists the way his father, Massasoit, had. He saw that the settlers were taking over his people's land and their traditional Indian hunting and fishing grounds. Soon after he came to power in 1664, King Philip began organizing his own military force. When English settlers tried and executed three of his warriors for the murder of another Indian, King Philip led an alliance of several tribes in a series of attacks against Massachusetts settlements. They burned houses and murdered colonists in frontier outpost towns such as Deerfield and Lancaster. The fighting continued over the next year, with many deaths on both sides. King Philip was hunted down and killed in December 1676, signaling defeat for the Wampanoags. Although they had won, the English settlers also paid a high price: The colony was in debt from the war, and more than 1,000 young men had died in battle.

Relations between the colonists and England became strained as well. At first, England left the colonies alone, and they thrived under their own government. But as the colonies became more prosperous and independent, the English government began protecting interests in the New World by creating the Navigation Acts, a series of laws passed between 1650 and 1773 designed to force the colonists to trade only with Britain. Shipping had been a vital Massachusetts industry since the 1630s, and the merchants did not want to be restricted. Many of them defied these new laws and turned to smuggling.

In an effort to regain control of its interests in the New World, England revoked the Massachusetts Bay Charter in 1684, and two years later appointed Sir Edmund Andros as Royal English governor of the Dominion of New England. The Dominion included Massachusetts Bay, Plymouth, Rhode Island, Connecticut, New Hampshire, and, later, New York and New Jersey. In 1691, Plymouth, Massachusetts Bay, and Maine were combined into one colony named Massachusetts. Puritan rule turned into British rule.

The Center of Resistance

During the 17th and 18th centuries, Britain was engaged in a struggle with France for control of America. The two nations fought in a series of conflicts known as the French and Indian Wars. French soldiers and their Indian allies frequently attacked settlements in Massachusetts. One of the most notorious incidents was a midnight raid on the town of Deerfield in 1704. Nearly 50 settlers were killed and more than 100 captured and held for ransom. The incident became known as the Deerfield Massacre. In the end, Britain won, and by 1763, the fighting had ended.

Britain taxed the colonies to pay for the French and Indian Wars. Some of the new taxes seemed unfair to the colonists, especially the Stamp Act of 1765, which taxed all printed matter, including newspapers and legal documents. Bostonians, angry about the new taxes, rioted in protest. They went so far as to attack Lieutenant Governor Thomas Hutchinson's house, leading the British crown to send in troops to keep order in the streets. Bostonians despised the presence of the British soldiers; scornful crowds threw icy snowballs at the red-coated soldiers they nicknamed "Lobster Backs."

On March 5, 1770, a group of British soldiers fired into a crowd, killing five and wounding others. The British captain later testified that the jeering crowd called out, "Come on you Rascals, you Bloody-backs, you Lobster Scoundrels; fire if you dare!" The event was used by Revolutionary leaders to stir up anti-British feeling among the colonists.

Another controversy was the Tea Act, passed by Parliament on April 27, 1773. The Tea Act allowed Britain's East India Company to sell its tea at a cheap rate. The colonists worried that this would hurt business for American tea merchants. When ships loaded with tea from the East India Company anchored in Boston Harbor, angry colonists who called themselves the Sons of Liberty staged a protest that became known as the Boston Tea Party. On December 16, 1773, Samuel Adams and other Sons of Liberty disguised themselves as Indians and dumped 342 chests of tea into Boston Harbor. To punish the colonists, Britain closed down the harbor and sent in a military governor, General Thomas Gage.

Britain's action united the colonists. Representatives from twelve colonies gathered in Philadelphia in the fall of 1774 for the First Continental Congress. They agreed to boycott (refuse to buy) British goods and planned to meet again. Meanwhile,

Paul Revere's engraving (above) shows British troops being ordered by their commander to fire at the colonists during the Boston Massacre. Although the exact story is unclear, Revere's engraving was widely circulated to fuel hatred against the Redcoats.

A common form of punishment in the colonies was to paint someone with sticky tar and then cover him with feathers. In this cartoon (right), patriotic colonists are forcing a British tax collector, whom they have tarred and feathered, to drink hot tea.

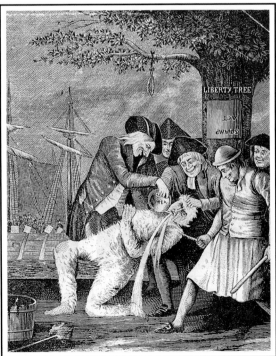

General Gage continued to gather his troops around Boston. Surrounding towns began to stockpile weapons for protection, readying themselves for battle.

British troops numbering nearly 800 set out on the evening of April 18, 1775, to raid a munitions stockpile believed to be in Concord. Paul Revere and others saddled up to sound the alarm that the British were coming. Civilians awoke and prepared for battle. These armed citizens became known as Minutemen because they were ready to fight at a moment's notice.

The next morning, a handful of armed villagers met Gage's troops at Lexington. After the Minutemen refused to put down their guns, shots were fired. Nobody knows which side fired the first shot, but the American Revolution had begun. Leaving eight dead and ten wounded, the Redcoats marched to Concord without much resistance and destroyed the weapons they found there.

The British had their first casualties in a fight with 400 Patriots at the Old North Bridge in Concord and began a retreat to Boston. On the way, however, colonists hiding behind trees and walls shot at the British almost continuously. By the time the Redcoats reached Boston, they had suffered more than 200 casualties.

The British were now trapped in Boston, held under siege by Patriot forces. Minutemen from other colonies came in to help with the siege,

which lasted almost a year. The Second Continental Congress met as planned, on May 10, 1775, and became the unofficial government of all thirteen colonies.

Britain sent nearly 6,000 reinforcements to Boston. The British stormed the Patriots' position atop Breed's Hill (known as the battle of Bunker Hill) on June 17. The Patriots pushed the Redcoats back twice. On the third try, the British broke through because the Patriots ran out of gun powder. Salem Poor, a black rifleman, was one Patriot to receive a reward for his bravery during the battle.

The Continental Army's luck began to change in March 1776 with the arrival of a supply of cannons that had been seized from the British. The

Patriots installed the cannons secretly at Dorchester Heights, and used the artillery to drive out thousands of British troops from Boston. This was the first major American victory of the war, and the last Revolutionary battle that was fought in Boston.

Samuel Adams, Paul Revere, and other Sons of Liberty disguised themselves as Mohawk Indians and came aboard East India tea ships on December 16, 1773. They dumped the tea cargo into Boston Harbor (opposite) as a protest against British taxation.

After British soldiers destroyed Concord's weapon supply, they were shot at by Minutemen all the way back to Boston (above). The Redcoats' bright uniforms and long marching lines made them easy targets for armed colonists hiding behind trees.

With the help of France, America defeated England on October 19, 1781, at Yorktown, Virginia. The thirteen colonies had won the fight for independence from Britain.

Immediately following the war, the new country experienced economic hardships. Crop prices fell, and paper money was almost worthless. Many farmers were in danger of losing their farms. When the governor raised taxes in 1786, Daniel Shays led a group of farmers in an armed rebellion, which shut down the Northampton, Worcester, and Springfield courthouses. The rebellion ended in 1787 when the "Shayites" surrendered.

Massachusetts citizens played a key role in the shaping of the new nation. John Adams, the nation's first vice president, helped write the state's constitution, which was a model for the United States Constitution and Bill of Rights. Massachusetts ratified the constitution in 1788, becoming the sixth state to join the Union.

John Adams (above, left) helped draft the Declaration of Independence as well as Massachusetts's state constitution. He was George Washington's vice president and became United States president himself in 1796.

This engraving (left) shows the rioters in Shays's Rebellion attacking the Springfield courthouse. Events like this convinced leaders of the need for a strong national government for the states.

A Fresh Start for Industry and Trade

After the Revolution, America needed to build a strong economy, and the key to growth and prosperity was the sea. Trade, shipbuilding, fishing, and whaling were the foundations upon which Massachusetts and the new nation would build. Sea merchants had used their vessels to fight the British during the war, and many ships had been damaged or lost in battle. Shipyards all along Massachusetts's coast quickly built and repaired American ships. In the 1780s, American merchants opened successful new trade routes to China, and Massachusetts shipbuilders, sea captains, and tradesmen all prospered.

Ships built in Massachusetts and New York helped the China trade grow. Because of its shipbuilding industry, Salem became America's main port for the China trade. Ships left Salem with cargo that included whale oil, tobacco, pottery, iron, and ale. The vessels sailed around Africa's Cape of Good Hope to China, often making three or four complete turnovers in cargo before returning home.

Massachusetts shipyards also supplied America's new navy. President George Washington and Congress ordered a new fleet to help sea merchants fight pirates off the coasts of Europe and Africa. In 1797, Boston launched one of the new ships, the U.S.S. *Constitution*, which came to be called "Old Ironsides."

Massachusetts's whaling industry also prospered during the first half of the 1800s. Whalers from New Bedford and Nantucket went on voyages that lasted two or three years at a time. As soon as a whale was sighted, the crew rowed out in small boats to spear the animal with harpoons. The crew would cut away its blubber, the thick fat under its skin, and boil it in huge kettles to make whale oil, which was used to light lamps and lubricate machinery. Whalebones became valuable in the making of umbrellas and ladies' corsets.

America's success at sea posed a threat to Britain. The British Royal Navy routinely seized American ships on their trade routes to France. In response, President Jefferson urged Congress to pass the Embargo Act in 1807. This law forbade American merchants to sell their goods to any other country. The president hoped that the embargo would hurt Britain and other European countries and force them to open their markets to fair trade.

The fight for control of the sea trade led to war in 1812. The people of Massachusetts opposed the war because it would put a halt to shipping, but conflict was inevitable. On

August 19, 1812, the U.S.S. *Constitution* defeated the British ship *Guerriere* in one of the war's most famous battles. Old Ironsides never lost a duel at sea and helped America fight to victory. The War of 1812 ended with the Treaty of Ghent, signed in 1814.

The 1812 conflict ushered in another wave of change for industry. During the war, America could not receive goods from other countries, and, as a result, Americans had to start making their own products.

Massachusetts became a leading manufacturer of cloth for the nation. Machines simplified the many steps involved in making cloth. A carding machine smoothed out the wool or cotton. Huge water-powered spinning machines replaced the spinning wheel for making yarn and thread. Boston's Francis Cabot Lowell and Paul Moody built the power loom, which could weave machine-spun yarn into cloth. These new inventions led to the construction of factories. Lowell's first textile factory opened in Waltham in 1814. For the first time, cloth could be made from start to finish by machines housed under one roof.

Lowell's factory used farm girls to change thread spools and cut cloth. By the 1830s, 85 percent of Lowell's workers were young women between the ages of fifteen and thirty. Lowell had to convince the girls' families that

At the end of the 18th century, Salem had become one of the richest ports in the nation, thanks to the China Trade. This illustration shows a typical trade ship (seen with its hold in cross section) as Salem wharf workers unload its cargo of luxuries from the Orient.

the work would not be dangerous, and that the girls would live in clean, well-supervised boarding houses. The girls would also be given schooling. Lowell's boarding houses offered libraries and free lectures.

Lowell's factories boomed. In 1823, he expanded his business and built huge mills along the banks of the Merrimack River. The city of Lowell became the first planned company town. Schools, churches, and stores were built for the workers. Every year, the City of Spindles, as it came to be known, made enough cloth to circle the globe twice.

By the middle of the 19th century, Massachusetts had become home to many other industries. Lawrence and Fall River sprouted textile mills. Worcester made paper. Springfield expanded its colonial firearms operations and housed the United States arsenal. Brockton, Lynn, and Haverhill used Elias Howe's new sewing machines to make shoes. By the turn of the century, more than half of America's shoes were made in Massachusetts. Many of these new factory jobs were filled by farmers who were having trouble making a living off the land. Farms were pushed farther west to the fertile Connecticut Valley or the Berkshire Hills, as the state changed from an agricultural to an industrial society.

This label of an early trademark of the Merrimack Manufacturing Company shows the power looms that made mass production of textiles possible. By 1836, the mills in Lowell were worth over $6 million.

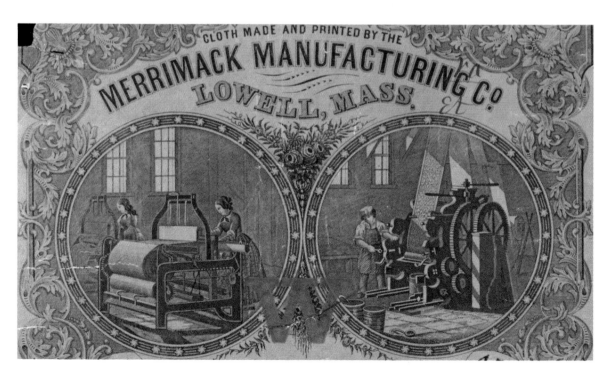

Abolition and the Civil War

Northern industry relied on paid laborers. The South, on the other hand, used slaves to do the work on farms and plantations. In the course of the 19th century, people in the North began to question the practice of slavery. Many felt that slavery should be limited, but only a small minority felt that it should be totally abolished. The people who wanted to end slavery were called abolitionists.

By the 1830s, most slaves lived in the Southern states. Although Massachusetts had abolished slavery in 1783, many people thought it was a necessary evil. Slavery was crucial to the Southern cotton industry, and textile mill owners in the North depended on the cotton to make and sell their cloth. Those who spoke against slavery were subject to attack and criticism.

The abolitionists were outspoken in their beliefs. One major Massachusetts abolitionist, William Lloyd Gar-

Slavery saw human beings as property, to be bought, sold, and traded like other material goods. This early engraving (top), showing a slave in chains, expresses the inhumanity of the practice.

William Lloyd Garrison (right) often faced attacks for his abolitionist views. On one occasion in 1835, he was tied up and dragged through the streets of Boston by an angry mob.

rison, faced the threat of death at the hands of angry mobs on more than one occasion in Boston. But he refused to back down. Garrison's antislavery newspaper, the *Liberator*, helped strengthen and increase the movement. The paper also helped the Massachusetts group unite with abolitionists elsewhere. With only a few thousand subscribers, the *Liberator* never made a profit, but its influence was great—many newspapers, North and South, printed stories that had first appeared in the *Liberator*.

Garrison and others organized the New England Antislavery Society in 1832. An escaped slave, Frederick Douglass, became a principal speaker for the group. "I appear this evening

as a thief and robber," Douglass often told his audiences, "I stole this head, these limbs, this body from my master, and ran off with them." The American Anti-Slavery Society formed the following year in Philadelphia, again with Garrison's help. This national group helped organize local chapters. They also sent letters and petitions to Congress, and passed out antislavery pamphlets in the slave states. The antislavery cause soon grew into a worldwide movement.

The heated debate over slavery continued to intensify. When fugitive slave Anthony Burns was arrested by federal officials in Boston in 1854, the trial became the most dramatic event of the year. When the court found in favor of Burns's master, church bells tolled and many buildings were draped in black. Thousands gathered along Boston's Long Wharf as Burns was marched to a ship bound for Richmond, Virginia. Troops and policemen had orders to shoot any citizen who interfered with his return to slavery.

Massachusetts citizens who were determined to fight slavery helped on the Underground Railroad, a network of reformers and freed slaves who helped fugitives get to Canada. Many ran railroad "depots," houses where slaves could hide until a transport could be arranged to take them north. Once across the border, these escaped slaves were less likely to be caught and returned to the South.

The slavery issue led to violence, even in Congress. In 1856 Massachusetts senator Charles Sumner spent two days criticizing the proslavery state of Missouri. In response, Congressman Preston S. Brooks of South Carolina took his cane and beat Sumner over the head until the abolitionist lay unconscious.

Clearly, it would take more than speeches and books to bring slavery to an end. So much tension built up between the North and the South that the Southern states threatened to withdraw (secede) from the union. In turn the north threatened war. South Carolina was the first Southern state to secede, in 1861, and the war between the states began.

None of the Civil War's battles took place in Massachusetts, but the state contributed a great deal to the effort. Springfield made thousands of rifles for the Union Army. Julia Ward Howe, poet and abolitionist, wrote the North's marching song, "The Battle Hymn of the Republic." Wounded soldiers called Massachusetts nurse Clara Barton "the Angel of the Battlefield." She drove supplies to the front lines by mule and wagon and went on to form the American Red Cross.

The slavery debate turned violent in Congress in 1856 when Representative Preston Brooks of South Carolina beat Massachusetts senator Charles Sumner with his walking stick (opposite).

Nurse Clara Barton (below) also helped gather identification of missing and dead soldiers during the Civil War.

When President Abraham Lincoln asked for volunteers to serve in the army, the Bay State was the first to answer. Massachusetts was also one of the first states to send an all-black regiment to fight, the 54th Massachusetts, led by Colonel Robert Gould Shaw. Sergeant William Carney, a member of the 54th, became the first of twenty-three African Americans to win the Congressional Medal of Honor.

The Civil War raged for four years. Over 600,000 Americans died in the conflict, the most in any American war. President Lincoln issued the Emancipation Proclamation in 1863, and slavery finally ended with the passage of the Thirteenth Amendment in 1865.

Massachusetts's all-black 54th regiment led the charge on Confederate Fort Wagner, in South Carolina, on July 18, 1863. Their leader, Colonel Robert Gould Shaw, who died in the battle, was the son of a Boston abolitionist family.

CHANGING TIMES

Rowes Wharf, built during a real estate boom in the 1980s, helped revitalize downtown Boston. Today, its shops and harbor promenade attract Bostonians and tourists alike.

The decades after the Civil War and into the 20th century were exciting and trying times for the Bay State. Massachusetts had established itself as an industrial and cultural leader. Boston particularly was a lively center for new literary and religious movements. But struggle lay ahead: The new century brought two world wars and the Great Depression. Changes in politics and society led to clashes between different groups of people. The challenge for the state's leaders lay in finding new solutions to these problems, and new sources of industry. Today, the innovative and expanding fields of computer technology and medicine are just two areas where the state is finding brighter hopes for the future.

"Hub of the Universe"

Massachusetts, and particularly Boston, became a center for new ideas and religious movements in the 19th century. Many important American writers, thinkers, and inventors came from the Boston area. This intellectual activity set Boston apart from other cities and earned it the nickname "Hub of the Universe."

Many new schools of religious thought were born in Massachusetts, such as the Universalist Church of America, formed in 1793, and the American Unitarian Association, founded in 1825. Unitarians believed in one God, but not the trinity of Father, Son, and the Holy Ghost. They also believed that people were essentially good, unlike the Puritans who believed that people were basically bad and needed the Puritan church in order to be saved. Both the Universalists and the Unitarians emphasized the worshipper's individual relationship with God; the church did not provide a list of religious rules for members to follow.

Mary Baker Eddy, a native of Amesbury, believed that sin and illness were illusions that could be overcome by mental concentration and a faith in God. Established churches, however, rejected her religious views. Eddy decided to start her own religion and founded the Church of Christ, Scientist, in Boston in 1879.

Transcendentalism, a philosophical movement that reached its peak in the 1840s, was greatly influenced by these new religious ideas. The transcendentalists believed that society restricted people's behavior too much, deciding how they should live and think. They believed that people should make up their own minds about right and wrong.

Ralph Waldo Emerson, a Unitarian minister, essayist, poet, and philosopher, was one of the leaders of transcendentalism. During the 1830s, Emerson shocked and inspired crowds that packed lecture halls to hear him speak. In his books and lectures, Emerson stressed the spiritual beauty of nature and the importance of the individual. Although some considered his views radical, Emerson had a large following and is considered to be one of the great American thinkers.

Another important figure in the transcendentalist movement was Henry David Thoreau. He believed that people should live as simply as possible and use their free time to learn from the natural world around them. Thoreau put his beliefs into practice by leaving Concord and building a small cabin on Walden Pond, where

This engraving (above) shows a Unitarian church in East Boston. Instead of being governed by a larger body, each Unitarian congregation had control over its own affairs.

Mary Baker Eddy (above, right), founder of the Christian Science movement, published many books and journals to lay down the doctrines of her faith. In 1908, she started the *Christian Science Monitor*.

This drawing (right) shows the cabin where Henry David Thoreau lived on Walden Pond for more than two years. He supported himself by tending a small vegetable garden and doing odd jobs in the village nearby.

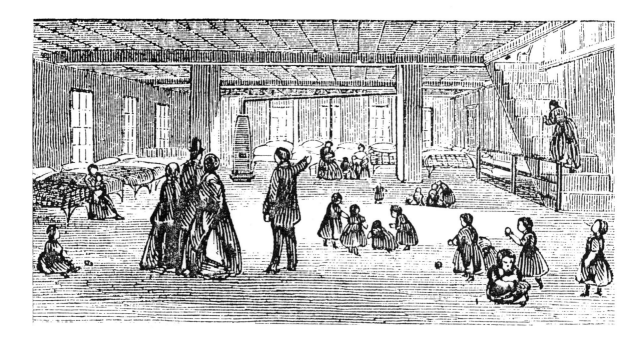

he lived for more than two years. He spent much of his time writing his observations of nature—reflections that were published as a book, *Walden*, in 1854.

What united these movements was a strong belief in human good. They inspired several reform groups to put these ideals into action. The reformers felt that poor people could succeed if they were given a fair chance by society. One Massachusetts reformer, Horace Mann, believed that all citizens in a democracy should be provided with free quality education. Mann improved the state's education system, working to provide better teachers and schools throughout Massachusetts. The nation's public school sys-

tem is based upon the successful changes Mann made in the Massachusetts schools. Other state reformers made their mark: Boston citizen Dorothea Dix helped prisoners and the mentally ill get better treatment, and Samuel Gridley Howe founded the Perkins School for the Blind in Brookline.

Scientists also thrived in Massachusetts at this time. Stockbridge native Cyrus Field developed the underground telegraph cable, eventually installing one across the Atlantic Ocean to Europe in 1866. Another revolutionary advance in communications came in 1876 when Alexander Graham Bell, a Boston professor, invented the telephone.

Sports and leisure expanded alongside the arts and sciences, and many important sports events took place in Massachusetts. Springfield's James Naismith invented basketball in 1891, and William G. Morgan of Holyoke started volleyball in 1895. In 1897, fifteen runners entered the first Boston Marathon. American baseball held the first World Series in Boston in 1903.

Growth in culture was matched by the growth of Massachusetts industry. During and after the Civil War, many changes took place. Cities on the Connecticut River in western Massachusetts, such as Chicopee, Holyoke, and Springfield, grew into large manufacturing centers. Two Springfield broth-

ers, Charles and Frank Duryea, made national news when they perfected the gasoline-powered car in 1892. Three years later in Springfield, they founded America's first automobile company. But not all Massachusetts industries continued to grow. Whaling declined after 1860 when kerosene replaced whale oil as a lighting fluid. As steamships became faster and safer,

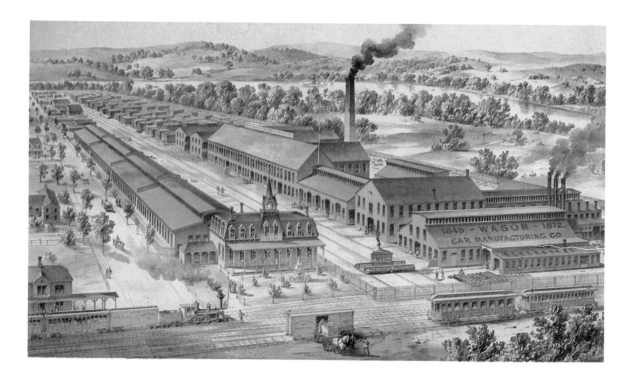

clipper ships disappeared as a means of transport.

The state's population grew as a result of industrial change. By mid-century, a great half-wheel of factory towns skirted Boston. When Boston ran out of space for its growing population, it simply filled in shallow coastal waterways with dirt and took over surrounding towns. These projects increased the size of the city thirty times between 1804 and 1858.

By 1855, almost one-third of Boston's population consisted of Irish immigrants who had come to America to escape Ireland's terrible potato famine. The newcomers arrived with little money and few possessions. They settled in crowded and unsanitary tenement houses. Irish immi-

Industry was not as heavy in the western part of Massachusetts as it was in the east, although Springfield was an important industrial center. The Wason Manufacturing Company of Springfield (above) built railway cars, supplying them to railroad companies across the nation.

grants worked in the mills, paved city streets, and built sewers, lights, canals, and railroads.

The Irish eventually gained power by working the political system to their advantage. Hugh O'Brien was elected Boston's first Irish mayor in 1884. Since then, almost all of Boston's mayors have been Irish. Patrick Joseph Kennedy was elected to the state senate in 1892. The Kennedy family would become a major presence in state and national politics in the later decades of the 20th century.

The Struggle for Rights

The Massachusetts labor force changed dramatically as immigrants replaced farm girls in the factories. They were Italians, Jews, Germans, Slavs, Poles, Portuguese, and French Canadians. Most newcomers did not speak English well, and at first they were relieved to find work of any kind. They accepted low pay, poor treatment, and miserable working conditions. But it wasn't long before the workers began to discuss the need for better working conditions. They formed unions to fight factory owners for more freedom, and discussed walking off the job (striking) to protest.

The 1912 textile strike in Lawrence, Massachusetts, was the most significant strike in the state's history. A national labor group, the Industrial Workers of the World (IWW), led the walkout. The struggle in Lawrence began over a wage cut. Young immigrant women, aged fourteen to eighteen, made up over half of the mills' labor force. Already suffering from

This view of Market Square (below) shows the cosmopolitan flavor of Boston in 1897. Waves of European immigrants in the late 19th century greatly changed Boston's ethnic mix as well as the character of its neighborhoods.

lack of food and sleep, the workers refused to accept another cut in pay. A group of about 100 women walked off the job. Two days later, on January 12, more than 20,000 workers joined them in a strike.

Local government and factory owners reacted violently to the strike, and the city called in state troops. After a female protester and a fifteen-year-old Syrian boy were killed in skirmishes on the picket lines, strikers began sending their children out of town. This called more attention to the strike. Local government officials declared that no more children could leave Lawrence, and when strikers defied the order and tried to send their children to safety, the police attacked them. People throughout the nation were horrified by the violence and sided with the strikers.

The strike succeeded. The unions and the owners reached a settlement in March. The workers earned wage increases, overtime pay, and other important gains.

Another major dispute in Massachusetts, the Boston Police Strike of 1919, helped turn the public against the labor movement. On September 8, a small group of Boston police officers were suspended from the force because they wanted to join the American Federation of Labor, a national labor organization. The next day, more than a thousand police walked off the job. With only a few hundred police left to protect the city, crime skyrocketed, and residents feared for their lives and safety.

The state sent in troops to restore order to the violent streets. Massachusetts governor Calvin Coolidge raged: "There is no right to strike against the public safety by anybody, anywhere, anytime." Coolidge refused to rehire the strikers, and the strike failed. His tough put-down of the walkout appealed to American voters who had grown fearful of the workers. These voters helped elect Coolidge as president in 1924.

Women also suffered inequality in the 19th and early 20th centuries. They had long been viewed as inferior to men. Although women had made gains in education and had entered the workforce in increasing numbers, they still faced limited opportunities at the turn of the century. For instance, women could not own property, and divorced mothers had no legal right to keep their children. More importantly, women were not allowed to vote, either in local or national elections.

Factory work in the late 19th century meant unsafe conditions and long working days— sometimes stretching as long as sixteen hours. This engraving (opposite, top), based on a drawing by Winslow Homer, shows workers— mainly women and children—leaving a textile mill at the end of the day.

The 1912 textile strike in Lawrence was a tense conflict between workers and authorities. This photograph (right) shows a group of textile workers, organized by the International Workers of the World, facing off with the state militia.

Women who worked in both the antislavery and labor movements were inspired to organize a movement for women's rights. Two Massachusetts natives, Lucy Stone and Lucretia Coffin Mott, became spokeswomen for the abolition of slavery and women's suffrage (the right to vote).

The first National Woman's Rights Convention was held in Worcester, Massachusetts, in 1850. Some newspapers made fun of the event. In response, women started their own newspapers to present their side of the story and advertise upcoming events. Susan B. Anthony published her paper, *Revolution*, in New York. Lucy Stone's *Woman's Journal* began in 1870 and continued publication for almost fifty years.

It would be seventy years before the nation accepted women's suffrage. Although Massachusetts led the nation in many areas of social change, it did not approve women's legal right to vote until 1920, the year the national law finally changed.

Governor Calvin Coolidge (below, left) won the antilabor vote when he broke the police strike of 1919. He went on to become president of the United States.

The League of Women Voters was founded to help women exercise their right to vote. The League published posters (below) and voting guides and sponsored public debates between the candidates.

League of Women Voters

Depression and Boom

The decades between 1900 and 1950 were difficult times for both Massachusetts and the nation. One factor was the growing popularity of socialism among workers and immigrants. Socialism was an idea for a new political system in which all property (factories, land, industries) would be owned and controlled by the people.

Many Americans felt threatened by socialism. Antisocialist feelings were strong in the Bay State as jobs became scarce after World War I. Many factory owners moved their industries to Southern states where the costs of doing business were lower. By the

Fear of foreigners grew after World War I. In one of the most controversial trials of the century, Sacco and Vanzetti (center) were convicted of murder. Many people felt they were denied a fair trial because they were immigrants.

1920s, hard times had hit Massachusetts, and immigrants were seen as a threat.

The United States government felt threatened by "reds" (as socialists were nicknamed) and conducted a series of raids, most of them in immigrant communities. Thousands of people were arrested during the nation's first "red scare."

Two Massachusetts Italians, Nicola Sacco and Bartolomeo Vanzetti, were afraid that they would be arrested for their political beliefs. They buried their political pamphlets and armed

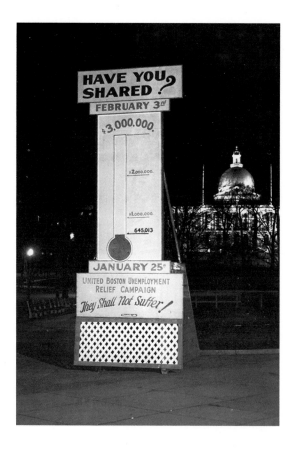

themselves with guns. On May 5, 1920, police arrested the two men, one a shoemaker, the other a fish peddler, and charged them with an armed robbery and murder that had taken place three weeks earlier.

For six years Sacco and Vanzetti and their supporters claimed that they were innocent. Many believed that they had been falsely convicted because they were Italian immigrants. But the governor disagreed and saw no need for another trial. On August 22, 1927, Sacco and Vanzetti were put to death by the electric chair in Charlestown, while protests raged around the world.

In 1929, a stock market crash plunged the entire nation into despair. Companies closed down, and workers lost their jobs. When the Depression of the 1930s hit, people all over the world suffered. Many Americans could not buy food, clothes, or pay their rent. Unemployment in some

During the Depression, Boston mayor James Michael Curley organized many fund-raisers for the city's poor. The capitol appears behind this display (above, left) on the Boston Common en-couraging citizens to contribute to the fund for the poor.

The Depression of the 1930s was the worst economic disaster the world has ever known. In this photograph (left), Bostonians wait in the bread lines that trailed along Hanover Street.

Fishing shacks and factory smokestacks stand side by side in this 1941 photograph (right) of New Bedford's waterfront. Mass production became commonplace during World War II.

areas of Massachusetts reached as high as 40 percent.

One Massachusetts leader, James Michael Curley, made a career out of trying to help the poorer residents of the city and state, particularly during the Depression. As mayor of Boston, he spent city funds to create jobs. Curley's colorful personality and ambitious programs made him a popular leader. In addition to four separate terms as mayor, Curley was twice elected to Congress and served as governor (1935–1937).

More relief came to the people of Massachusetts with President Franklin D. Roosevelt's New Deal programs. These were federal laws that provided loans for houses and new jobs building schools and roads. The New Deal helped the people of Massachusetts get back on their feet.

Complete economic recovery for the nation and the state came with World War II. America entered the war on December 7, 1941, when the Japanese bombed Pearl Harbor. U.S. troops needed weapons, aiplanes, and ships. Massachusetts factories produced radar, sonar, and airplane engines. Decaying shipyards at Quincy and Lynn sprang back to life. The growth of all of these industries led to a boom in the state's economy.

The war brought new opportunities for black workers. Hundreds of thousands of African Americans moved to New England from the South to work in weapons plants. Many blacks faced unfair treatment, however, often

receiving less pay than white workers for the same jobs.

Millions of American women also joined the workforce as men left to fight overseas, learning new skills in the defense plants. Before the war, women had been barred from working in heavy industry. With World War II, welding, aircraft assembly, and tool and die making were open to women.

Scientists at the nation's universities also played an important role during the war by inventing new weapons and equipment. Both the Massachusetts Institute of Technology (MIT) and Harvard became important resource centers for the nation. MIT helped develop radar, which could spot enemy aircraft and ships more

These giant gears (above) were made in Massachusetts during World War II for American warships. Wartime industries such as shipbuilding and scientific research and development brought prosperity to the state.

quickly. Radar also revolutionized aviation and led to the creation of a major industry for America.

Medical advances were also important to the war effort. Research at Harvard Medical School led to the making and use of dried blood plasma, which saved many soldiers' lives on the battlefield.

Massachusetts industry had recovered from the Depression. The economic foundation built during World War II continued to support the state in the following years.

Tides of Change

The technological innovations developed by Massachusetts universities during World War II led to new jobs and businesses in the state. Scientists at MIT, among other schools, worked on the research that led to the development of new products such as computers, hand-held calculators, and medical equipment. Business people then started companies to make and sell these high-tech products. Many of the electronics companies built their offices along Route 128, a highway located west of Boston that became known as "America's Technology Highway."

Tourism also became an important industry in Massachusetts after World War II. Hikers enjoyed the mountains in the Berkshires. Lenox, Lee, Great Barrington, and Stockbridge have grown to become popular Berkshire mountain resort towns both in summer and winter. Since 1934, music lovers have attended Tanglewood Music Festival in the Berkshires. The beaches and historic homes and muse-

Each summer, thousands are drawn to the outdoor Tanglewood Music Festival in Lenox (above, right). The popular Berkshire county event includes classical, folk, rock, and jazz performances.

Polaroid founder Edward H. Land (right) unveils a photograph of himself using the one-step, develop-and-print process that changed photography. The company made its first sale in 1947 and became a large Massachusetts employer.

ums of Nantucket, Cape Cod, and Martha's Vineyard are all popular spots for tourists. Boston's rich assortment of museums, historic buildings, trails, and monuments has also drawn out-of-towners from all over.

The city of Boston underwent changes after World War II. Many residents left Boston for the suburbs. To encourage people to move back, city planners decided to give Boston a facelift. Between 1960 and 1968, Mayor John F. Collins led the ambitious program. Many new buildings changed the city's skyline. The sixty-acre Government Center complex, designed by noted architect I. M. Pei, replaced a seedy and run-down section of town called Scollay Square.

Mayor Kevin H. White, elected in 1967, continued Collins's program. The sheer glass Hancock Tower and the Federal Reserve Bank Building are two of the forty new buildings constructed during White's sixteen years as mayor. Some voters criticized White in later years for putting business needs ahead of the needs of neighborhood residents. White's opponents claimed he was destroying old neighborhoods for the sake of business profit. Other citizens benefited from the new jobs created by his programs.

The state came to political prominence on the national level when voters across the nation elected John F. Kennedy as the thirty-fifth president of the United States in 1960. The youngest president in history, he inspired the nation in his inaugural address to "Ask not what your country can do for you—ask what you can do for your country." Throughout his political career, Kennedy worked for progressive health, housing, and civil rights programs. The Brookline native and Harvard graduate represented Massachusetts for three terms in the House of Representatives (1946–52) and in the Senate (1952–60). Kennedy was the first Catholic to be elected president.

The president's brothers, Robert and Edward, also succeeded in politics. Robert Kennedy served as attorney general in the Kennedy administration. Two of the brothers were assassinated—John in 1963 and Robert in 1968. Younger brother Edward (Teddy) Kennedy remained politically active as the longest-serving United States senator in the history of Massachusetts.

Economic hard times hit the region in the 1970s. Cities across the country faced problems of racism, poverty, and decay. In Boston the ethnic mix of neighborhoods such as Mattapan, North Dorchester, Roxbury, and Jamaica Plain changed rapidly as African Americans, Hispanics, and Asians moved in. Area residents felt pushed out by the newcomers.

By the late 1960s, the condition of inner city neighborhoods and schools had deteriorated. At that time, black students went to all-black neighbor-

The Kennedy family, like the Adams family of the Revolutionary Era, profoundly affected state and national politics. This photo (above) of the Kennedy clan was taken in Hyannis Port in the early 1960s. Teddy (holding his children) and Bobby (kneeling, in dark sweater) are in the back row; John (with hands clasped) sits just right of center.

During his campaign and presidency, John Kennedy relied on the council and support of his brother Bobby. In this photograph (right), the Kennedys await word of John's nomination at the Democratic National Convention, 1960.

hood schools and white students went to all-white neighborhood schools. Many all-black schools had broken windows, poor lighting, poor heating, and outdated textbooks. Civil rights leaders pushed for laws that would bus black children to white schools, and vice versa, hoping that black students would get a better education in an integrated school system.

On June 21, 1974, state judge Arthur Garrity ordered that busing begin on September 12. Board of Education officials took a map of Boston and divided it into districts so that each school would have an equal balance of black and white students.

Many neighborhoods rejected the decision and greeted bused black students with racist shouts and flying bottles. In December a seventeen-year-old white boy was stabbed by a black student at South Boston High School. The protest gradually died down. Some white families moved out of the city altogether; others sent their children to private schools.

In addition to troubling race relations, many Massachusetts residents faced troubling economic times and lost their jobs during the recession of the mid-1970s. In 1975, Boston's unemployment rate stood at 12.8 percent, quite a bit higher than the national rate of 8.5 percent.

After being elected governor in 1974, Michael S. Dukakis raised taxes and cut spending on social programs. The increase in taxes earned the state the nickname "Taxachusetts." Duk-

akis lost his reelection bid in 1974 but won two more terms from 1982–90.

Many industries moved to Massachusetts during the 1980s, creating jobs. By 1988, unemployment had fallen and personal incomes had increased. Dukakis ran on the Democratic ticket for the presidency in 1988, claiming credit for the economic success of the state, which he called the "Massachusetts Miracle."

The "Miracle" turned out to be short-lived. Few of the businesses that had made money continued to prosper in the 1990s. The computer industry shrank, the real estate market crashed, and local banks failed. Massachusetts was not alone: Many states struggled with difficult economic challenges as they entered the 1990s.

White students and parents reacted violently to court-ordered school integration in the 1970s. In this Pulitzer Prize-winning photograph (opposite), high school students from South Boston attack a black man outside city hall.

Children, both black and white, were affected by the busing experiment of the 1970s. This photograph (above, right) shows white children getting off a bus to attend the Lee School, in a mostly black Boston neighborhood.

Michael Dukakis (the "Duke") ran against then-Vice President George Bush in the 1988 presidential campaign. He lost to the Republicans despite his promise to deliver a national turnaround similar to his "Massachusetts Miracle." This button (right) is from his campaign.

A Promising Future

The future holds the promise of economic recovery in Massachusetts. In the early 1990s health care, education, and biotechnology were the state's strongest industries.

Massachusetts has always been a world leader in health care, because of its many teaching hospitals and medical research facilities. Medical professionals in the state have been at the center of the many debates about national health care. Massachusetts was one of the states that pioneered Health-Maintenance Organizations (HMOs), which focus on keeping people well rather than just treating the sick.

Education has always been an important business in the Bay State. The state hosts more than 100 colleges and universities, and the Boston area has become one of the world's great education centers. The city's population swells by some 250,000 students each school year. Five respected colleges are located in the western part of the state; the University of Massachusetts, Hampshire College, Amherst College, Smith College, and Mount Holyoke.

Biotechnology—the industrial use of biological knowledge—is a growing business in Massachusetts. This involves genetic engineering—the use of plant and animal genes in custom-designed foods, drugs, and fertilizers.

I. M. Pei's glassy John Hancock Tower reflects nearby Trinity Church in Boston's Copley Square. The architect's design captures the historic nature of Boston as a base from which to reach toward the future.

Scientists, for example, have used genetic engineering to make a stronger corn seed. They hope to develop corn that will become so strong that no drought, insect, worm, or chemical can kill it.

State officials are working hard to encourage biotech companies to build their manufacturing plants in Massachusetts, joining those already located in Worcester, Boston, and Cambridge.

Hazardous waste cleanup for areas damaged by pollution is another growing business in the state. Hazardous waste and other environmental problems are particularly bad in the Northeast. Companies have been dumping chemicals, dyes, and waste into rivers since the first textile and

paper mills appeared in the early 19th century. Many of Massachusetts's rivers were terribly polluted, especially the Merrimack and Nashua rivers. Fish that used to populate the waterways had died off, and people were not allowed to swim in the water. No laws existed in the 1960s to keep factories from dumping toxic waste into rivers. Environmental groups such as the Nashua River Watershed Association fought for legislation to clean up the rivers.

Massachusetts voters passed the state's Clean Water Act in 1966. The law forced factories along the state's rivers to dispose of industrial waste in other ways. The rivers responded to these environmental efforts dramatically. Within a few years, the Nashua and Merrimack rivers were again alive with fish. The state proved that serious cleanup efforts can succeed.

Massachusetts residents hoped that the clean-up of Boston Harbor, the most polluted waterway in America, would be successful. Since the 1890s, Boston had been dumping sewage into the Atlantic Ocean. Although the sewage system had been updated, waste still flowed right into the sea, only one mile from shore.

Boston officials tried to ignore the problem, in spite of complaints about the filth that washed up on the beaches. One city official, William Golden, encountered the problem himself while jogging along the beach in Quincy one morning in 1982. Golden and other officials and citizens started lawsuits and made proposals to clean up Boston Harbor. Their work led to the founding of the Massachusetts Water Resources Authority (MWRA) in 1984. Clean-up of Boston Harbor and improvements to the state's sewage system were well under way when the 1990s began.

Massachusetts citizens have enjoyed a long history of success based on their ability to think of new ideas and solutions to problems. Environmental problems and economic hardships are ongoing. Massachusetts once again has the power to lead the nation to change—this time toward a healthier environment and an economy based on the needs of peace, not war.

Laboratory technicians analyze the results of a biotechnology experiment in this photograph (opposite). Biotechnology is a growing and profitable industry for Massachusetts.

Water pollution has been a problem in Massachusetts since the first mills of the early 19th century. Environmental cleanup efforts have been able to restore the delicate ecosystems and natural beauty to many of the state's waterways and rivers (below).

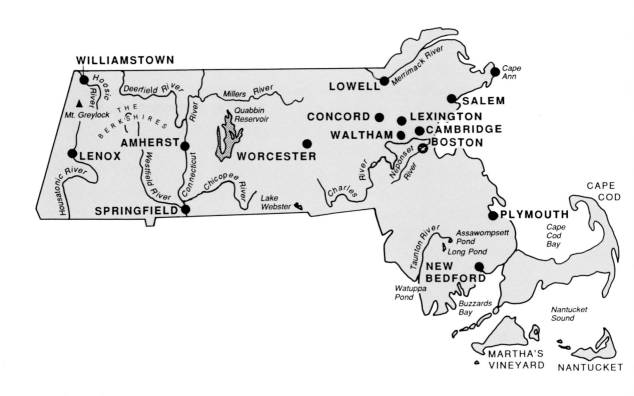

Land area:
   8,284 square miles, of which 460 are inland water. Ranks 45th in size.

Major rivers:
   The Connecticut; the Hoosic; the Housatonic; the Merrimack; the Blackstone; the Taunton; the Charles; the Neponset.

Highest point:: Mt. Greylock, 3,487 ft.

Major bodies of water:
   Assawompsett Pond; Watuppa Pond; Long Pond; Lake Webster; Quabbin Reservoir.

Climate:
   Average January temperature: 30° F (Boston); 21° F (Pittsfield)
   Average July temperature: 74° F (Boston); 68° F (Pittsfield)

Population: 6,016,425 (1990)
Rank: 13th
    1900: 2,805,346
    1790: 378,787

Population of major cities (1992):

Boston	574,283
Worcester	169,759
Springfield	156,983
Lowell	103,439
New Bedford	99,922
Cambridge	95,802

Ethnic breakdown by percentage (1990):

White	87.8%
Hispanic	4.8%
African American	4.6%
Asian	2.3%
Native American	0.2%
Other	0.3%

Economy:
    Manufacturing (electric and electronic equipment, machinery, technical and scientific instruments); finance; real estate; insurance; trade; transportation; communications; fishing; tourism; agriculture; mining.

State government:
    Legislature: Made up of the 40-member Senate and the 160-member House of Representatives. Both senators and representatives serve 2-year terms.
    Governor: The governor, who is elected to a 4-year term, heads the executive branch.
    Courts: Massachusetts consists of 14 counties. The supreme judicial court is the highest court in the state. It has a chief justice and six associate justices.
State capital: Boston

State Flag

The Massachusetts state flag shows a Native American holding a bow and arrow in the center of a blue shield. The state motto appears on the banner that flows around the shield. This version of the flag was adopted in 1971.

State Seal

Massachusetts's state seal, adopted in 1885, carries the same symbols as the state flag. The white star in the upper left is a reminder that Massachusetts was one of the original thirteen colonies.

State Motto

Massachusetts's motto, "Ense petit placidam sub libertate quietem," means: "By the sword we seek peace, but peace only under liberty."

State Nickname

"The Bay State."

Places

Adams National Historic Site, Quincy

American Jewish Historical Society, Brandeis University, Waltham

Armenian Library Museum of America, Waltham

Arnold Arboretum, Jamaica Plain

Black Heritage Trail, Boston

Bunker Hill Monument, Charlestown

Cape Cod National Seashore, Cape Cod

Children's Museum, Boston

Computer Museum, Boston

DeCordova Museum and Sulpture Park, Lincoln

Denison House, Dorchester

Drumlin Farm, Lincoln

Essex Institute, Salem

Fenway Park, Boston

Freedom Trail, Boston

Habitat Institute for the Environment, Belmont

Historic Deerfield, Deerfield

House of the Seven Gables, Salem

Institute of Contemporary Art, Boston

John F. Kennedy Library, Dorchester

Longfellow National Historic Site, Cambridge

Lowell National Historical Park, Lowell

to See

Minute Man National Historical Park, Concord

Museum of Afro-American History, Boston

Museum of Fine Arts, Boston

Museum of Science, Boston

Basketball Hall of Fame, Springfield

Whaling Museum, New Bedford

New England Aquarium, Boston

The Old Schwamb Mill, Arlington

Old Sturbridge Village, Sturbridge

Orchard House, Concord

Peabody Museum, Salem

Plimouth Plantation, Plymouth

Plum Island National Wildlife Refuge, Newburyport

Ralph Waldo Emerson House, Concord

Sandwich Glass Museum, Sandwich

Salem Maritime National Historic Site, Salem

Saugus Iron Works, Saugus

Tanglewood Music Festival, Lenox

USS Constitution, Charlestown

Wampanoag Indian Reservation, Martha's Vineyard

Whaling Museum, Nantucket

Woods Hole Oceanographic Institute, Cape Cod

Worcester Art Museum, Worcester

State Flower

The mayflower, or trailing arbutus, is a slow-growing evergreen that bears fragrant white or pink flowers in the spring. The flower, probably named for the famous Pilgrim ship, was officially adopted on May 1, 1918.

State Bird

The chickadee was named Massachusetts's official bird in 1941. This tiny half-ounce bird, named for its call: "chick-a-dee-dee," can even be tamed to eat out of the human hand.

State Tree

The American elm was officially adopted in 1941 in memory of the first Liberty Tree that stood in the Boston Common during colonial times.

Massachusetts History

1500s Indian tribes settled in region include the Massachusets, Nausets, Nipmucs, Pennacooks, Pocomtucs, and Wampanoags

1602 Bartholomew Gosnold explores the region

1614 Captain John Smith maps New England

1620 Pilgrims found Plymouth

1621 Pilgrims and Indians celebrate first Thanksgiving

1630 Puritans settle in Boston area

1675–76 Colonists defeat Indians in King Philip's War

1691 Massachusetts becomes a royal British colony

1704 America's first successful newspaper, *The Boston News-Letter*, begins

1770 Five colonists killed in the Boston Massacre

1773 Boston Tea Party

1775 The American Revolutionary War begins with battles at Lexington and Concord

1780 State constitution approved

1788 Massachusetts becomes the 6th state of the Union

1806 The first church built by free blacks, African Meeting House, opens in Boston

1814 Francis Cabot Lowell opens textile factory in Waltham

1826 First American railroad built in Quincy

American

1492 Christopher Columbus reaches America

1607 Jamestown (Virginia) founded by English colonists

1620 *Mayflower* arrives at Plymouth (Massachusetts)

1754–63 French and Indian War

1765 Parliament passes Stamp Act

1775–83 Revolutionary War

1776 Signing of the Declaration of Independence

1788–90 First congressional elections

1791 Bill of Rights added to U.S. Constitution

1803 Louisiana Purchase

1812–14 War of 1812

1820 Missouri Compromise

1836 Battle of the Alamo, Texas

1846–48 Mexican-American War

1849 California Gold Rush

1860 South Carolina secedes from Union

1861–65 Civil War

1862 Lincoln signs Homestead Act

1863 Emancipation Proclamation

1865 President Lincoln assassinated (April 14)

1865–77 Reconstruction in the South

1866 Civil Rights bill passed

1881 President James Garfield shot (July 2)

History

1896 First Ford automobile is made

1898–99 Spanish-American War

1901 President William McKinley is shot (Sept. 6)

1917 U.S. enters World War I

1922 Nineteenth Amendment passed, giving women the vote

1929 U.S. stock market crash; Great Depression begins

1933 Franklin D. Roosevelt becomes president; begins New Deal

1941 Japanese attack Pearl Harbor (Dec. 7); U.S. enters World War II

1945 U.S. drops atomic bomb on Hiroshima and Nagasaki; Japan surrenders, ending World War II

1963 President Kennedy assassinated (November 22)

1964 Civil Rights Act passed

1965–73 Vietnam War

1968 Martin Luther King, Jr., shot in Memphis (April 4)

1974 President Richard Nixon resigns because of Watergate scandal

1979–81 Hostage crisis in Iran: 52 Americans held captive for 444 days

1989 End of U.S.-Soviet cold war

1991 Gulf War

1993 U.S. signs North American Free Trade Agreement with Canada and Mexico

Massachusetts History

1831 Abolitionists start antislavery newspaper, *The Liberator*

1850 America's first women's suffrage convention held in Worcester

1876 Alexander Graham Bell patents the telephone

1897 Boston opens the nation's first subway

1912 Textile strike in Lawrence

1919 The National Guard is called in to end Boston's Police Strike

1927 Sacco and Vanzetti executed

1928 MIT develops the first computer

1940 Microwave radar developed at MIT

1957 Massachusetts Turnpike opened

1959 First nuclear powered submarine launched at Quincy

1960 Brookline-born John F. Kennedy elected president

1974 Busing ordered to desegregate Boston schools

1980 Tax-cutting measure Proposition 2½ passed

1988 Governor Michael Dukakis runs for president on the Democratic ticket

1990 William Weld is the first Republican elected governor since 1975

1990s Massachusetts undertakes cleanup of Boston Harbor, the country's most polluted waterway

Massasoit (1580–1661)
This Wampanoag chief remained a loyal and peaceful friend of the Pilgrims. He joined the first Thanksgiving with the Pilgrims. However, his son **Metacomet (King Philip; 1639?–76)** chose to wage war with the colonists. King Philip's War ended after one year with a defeat for the Indians.

Benjamin Franklin

Squanto (1585?–1622)
Squanto taught the colonists where to find food and how to plant corn. In 1619, he acted as interpreter for the Plymouth settlers during negotiations with Massasoit.

John Winthrop (1588–1649) Winthrop was leader of the first Puritans to settle in Massachusetts and served four terms as governor.

Benjamin Franklin (1706–90) Franklin is famous for his early experiments with electricity. As a statesman, he helped draft the Declaration of Independence and the U.S. Constitution.

Samuel Adams (1722–1803) A patriot and politician, Adams was a key figure in the fight for America's independence from Britain. He was a founder of the Sons of Liberty and organized the Boston Tea Party.

John Adams (1735–1826) Adams became the second president of the United States in 1797. He helped draft the Declaration of Independence and the Massachusetts state constitution. His wife **Abigail Smith Adams (1744–1818)** was a lifelong feminist whose letters helped document the Revolutionary War. Their son, **John Quincy Adams (1767–1848),** was secretary of state before he became the sixth president of the United States.

Phillis Wheatley (1753?–84) A slave educated by her owner, Wheatley began writing poetry at age thirteen. She is now recognized as the country's first notable African-American poet.

Francis Cabot Lowell (1775–1817) An industrialist, Lowell founded the first textile mill in Waltham in 1814. He built the mill town of Lowell, Massachusetts.

Ralph Waldo Emerson (1803–82) This philosopher developed transcendentalism and became an influential and popular poet, essayist, and lecturer.

Nathaniel Hawthorne (1804–64) One of America's celebrated novelists, Hawthorne wrote *The Scarlet Letter,* set in colonial times.

Lucy Stone (1818–93) Dedicated to the antislavery and women's rights movements, Stone organized the

Phillis Wheatley

American Women's Suffrage Association in 1869.

Clara Barton (1821–1912)
A nurse during the Civil War, Barton was called "the angel of the battlefield." She founded the American Red Cross.

Louisa May Alcott (1832–88) Alcott's novels of family life in Concord, *Little Women* and its sequels, became children's classics.

Emily Dickinson (1830-86) Called "the Belle of Amherst," Dickinson is hailed today as one of America's finest poets.

Calvin Coolidge (1872–1933) After serving one term as governor of Massachusetts, Coolidge became the thirtieth president of the United States in 1923.

Robert Hutchings Goddard (1882–1945) Goddard laid the grounds for modern rocket technology when he fired the world's first successful liquid-propellant rocket in 1926.

Bette Davis (1908–89) A native of Lowell, Davis went on to become one of Hollywood's biggest stars during the 1930s and 1940s. She won Academy awards for her performances in *Dangerous* and *Jezebel* and was famous for her portrayal of strong women.

Thomas P. (Tip) O'Neill (1912–94) A native of Cambridge, O'Neill represented Massachusetts in Congress for over thirty years. As Speaker of the House (1976–86), O'Neill was a powerful Democratic leader in national politics.

John Fitzgerald Kennedy (1917–63) From a long line of Massachusetts politicians, Kennedy became America's thirty-fifth president. He was assassinated in 1963. His brother **Robert Francis Kennedy (1925–68)** was assassinated five years later while campaigning for the Democratic presidential nomination. He had served as U.S. attorney general. A younger brother, **Edward Moore (Teddy) Kennedy (b. 1932)** served the most terms in the U.S. Senate in the history of Massachusetts.

Edward William Brooke (b. 1919) As attorney general of Massachusetts, Brooke gained national attention for exposing a corrupt state government. In 1967, he became

Tip O'Neill

the first African American to be elected to the Senate since Reconstruction.

An Wang (1920–90) Wang invented the first successful memory storage device used in computers before the invention of the microchip.

Jack Kerouac (1922–68) Author of the novel, *On the Road*, this Lowell native was a spokesman for the Beat Generation, a social and literary movement of the 1950s.

George Herbert Walker Bush (b. 1924) Born in Milton, Bush became the forty-first president of the United States in 1988. He also served as director of the CIA and vice president for two terms.

RESOURCE GUIDE

Pictures in this volume:

Amherst College: 2

Biogen: 52

Boston Public Library, Print Dept.: 42 (both), 49

Boston Symphony Orchestra: 45

Dover Pictures: 10 (both)

I.M. Pei Architects: 50

J. F. Kennedy Library: 47 (top)

Library of Congress: 7, 9 (both), 11, 12, 15, 17, 19 (both), 21, 22 (bottom), 27 (both), 28, 29, 30, 33 (all), 34, 35, 36, 37, 39 (bottom), 40 (both), 41, 43, 47 (bottom), 60 (both), 61

Massachusetts Office of Travel & Tourism: 31

Massachusetts Secretary of State: 56 (both), 57

Museum of American Textile History: 26

National Archives: 44

National Park Service: 24

Plimouth Plantation: 13

Polaroid Corporation: 45

Private Collection: 10 (bottom), 20, 49, 53

Stanley Forman: 48

About the author:

Monique Avakian is a Boston-based freelance writer and editor. She attended Beloit College in Wisconsin, where she won the Von Eschen-Steele award for excellence in education. Her nonfiction books include: *The Meiji Restoration* and *The Rise of Modern Japan* (Silver Burdett & Ginn), and *A Historical Album of New York* (The Millbrook Press).

Suggested reading:

Buyers, Helen, *Kidding Around Boston, A Young Person's Guide*, Santa Fe: John Muir Publications, 1990, 1993

Fradin, Dennis B., *The Massachusetts Colony*, Chicago: Childrens Press, 1987

Kent, Deborah, *America the Beautiful: Massachusetts*, Chicago: Childrens Press, 1987

Kent, Zachary, *Cornerstones of Freedom: The Story of the Salem Witch Trials*, Chicago: Childrens Press, 1987

Waters, Kate, *Sarah Morton's Day: A Day in the Life of a Pilgrim Girl*, New York: Scholastic Inc., 1989

For more information contact:

Massachusetts Historical Society
1154 Boylston Street
Boston, MA 02116
Tel. (617) 536-1608

Massachusetts Office of Travel and Tourism
100 Cambridge Street, 13th Floor
Boston, MA 02202
Tel. (617) 727-3201

INDEX

Page numbers in *italics* indicate illustrations

abolitionists, *27*, *28*, 29, 40
Adams, Abigail Smith, 60
Adams, John, *22*, 60
Adams, John Quincy, 60
Adams, Samuel, 18, 21, 60
Alcott, Louisa May, 61
Algonquian, 8
American Anti-Slavery Society, 28
Andros, Edmund, 17
Anthony, Susan B., 40
automobile industry, 35

Barton, Clara, *29*, 61
"Battle Hymn of the Republic, The," 29
Bay Psalm Book, *15*
Bell, Alexander Graham, 34, *35*
biotechnology, 50, *52*
bird, state, *57*
blacks
  abolitionist, 28
  in Civil War, *30*
  in labor force, 43-44
  in Revolutionary War, 21
  and school busing, *48*, *49*
  segregation of, 46, 48
  See also slavery
Boston, Massachusetts, 32, *37*, *50-51*, 52
  Depression in, *42*, 43
  downtown renewal in, *31*, 46
  education in, 15, 48, *49*, 50
  founding of, 14
  fugitive slave in, 28-29
  inner city, 46
  Irish immigrants in, 36
  Marathon, 35
  Massacre, 18, *19*
  nickname of, 14
  police strike in, 38
  population of, 36, 55
  in Revolutionary War, 20-21
  Stamp Act riots in, 18
  Tea Party, 18, *20*, 21
  water pollution in, 53
Britain
  embargo of, 23
  explorers, 11
  Navigation Acts, 17
  Puritans and, 13
  in Revolutionary War, 20, *21*, 22
  taxes on colonies, 18, *19*
  in War of 1812, 23-24
Brockton, Massachusetts, 26
Brooke, Edward William, 61
Brooks, Preston, *28*, 29
Bunker Hill, Battle of, 21
Burns, Anthony, 28-29
Bush, George, 61

Cambridge, Massachusetts, 15, 52, 55

Canada, 10, 29
canoe, 8
Cape Cod, 8, *11*, 12, 46
Carney, William, 30
Champlain, Samuel de, 10
Charles I, King, 13
Chicopee, Massachusetts, 35
China trade, 23
Civil War, 29, *30*
Clean Water Act, 52-53
Collins, John F., 46
Concord, Massachusetts, 20, 32
Congress, U.S., 23, *28*, 29
Congressional Medal of Honor, 30
Connecticut, 15, 16, 17
constitution, state, 22
Constitution, USS, 23, 24
Continental Army, 21
Continental Congress, 18, 21
Coolidge, Calvin, 38, *40*, 61
corn, 8, *9*
Cotton, John, 14
Curley, James Michael, 42, 43
Cuttyhunk Island, 11

Davis, Bette, 61
Daye, Stephen, 15
Deerfield Massacre, 18
Depression, *42*, 43
Dickinson, Emily, 61
disease, Native American, 8, 14
Dix, Dorothea, 34
Dominion of New England, 17
Douglass, Frederick, 28
Dukakis, Michael S., 48-49, *50*
Duryea, Charles and Frank, 35

economy, 42-43, 48-49, 50, 55
Eddy, Mary Baker, 32, *33*
education
  busing, 48, *49*
  Puritan, 15
  reform, 34, *35*
  segregated, 46, 48
Elizabeth Islands, 11
Emancipation Proclamation, 30
Embargo Act, 23
Emerson, Ralph Waldo, 32, 60
Ericson, Leif, 10
explorers, 10, *11*

factories, 24, 26, 37-38
Fall River, Massachusetts, 26
farming
  decline of, 26
  Native American, 8, *9*
  in Plymouth Colony, 14
  Shay's Rebellion, *22*
Field, Cyrus, 34
fishing, 8, 14, 23
flag, state, *56*
flower, state, *57*

food, 8, 12, 14
Fort Wagner, *30*
France, 10, 18, 22
Franklin, Benjamin, *60*
French and Indian Wars, 18
fur trade, 11

Gage, Thomas, 18, 20
Garrison, William Lloyd, *27*, 28
Garrity, Arthur, 48
Goddard, Robert Hutchings, 61
Golden, William, 53
Gosnold, Bartholomew, *11*
Guerriere, 24

harpoons, *7*, 8, 23
Harvard University, 15, 44
Haverhill, Massachusetts, 26
Hawthorne, Nathaniel, 60
hazardous waste, 52
Health-Maintenance Organizations (HMOs), 50
Holyoke, Massachusetts, 35
houses
  Native American, 8, *9*
  in Plymouth Colony, 13
Howe, Elias, 26
Howe, Julia Ward, 29
Howe, Samuel Gridley, 34
hunting, 8, 14
Hutchinson, Thomas, 18

immigrants, 36, 37, 41-42
Industrial Workers of the World (IWW), 37, 38
industry
  automobile, 35
  biotechnology, 50, *52*
  centers of, 35, *36*
  decline of, 49
  high-tech, 45, 49
  shipbuilding, 23, 36
  shoe, 26
  textile, 24, 26, 27
  tourism, *45*, 46
  in wartime, 43, *44*
  whaling, *7*, 24, 35
  See also labor force
Irish immigrants, 36

James I, King, 13
Jamestown, Virginia, 11
Jefferson, Thomas, 23

Kennedy, Edward M., 46, *47*, 61
Kennedy family, *47*
Kennedy, John F., 46, *47*, 61
Kennedy, John Patrick, 36
Kennedy, Robert, 46, *47*, 61
Kerouac, Jack, 61
King Philip's War, 16, *17*, 60

labor force
  immigrants in, 37
  women in, 24, 26, 37-38, *39*
Land, Edward H., *45*
Lawrence, Massachusetts, 26, 37-38, *39*
League of Women Voters, *40*
Lexington, Massachusetts, 20
Liberator, 28
Lincoln, Abraham, 30
Lowell, Francis Cabot, 24, 26, 60
Lowell, Massachusetts, 26, 55
Lynn, Massachusetts, 26

Maine, 15, 17
Mann, Horace, 34
Martha's Vineyard, 8, 11, 46
Mashpee, 8
Massachusetts Bay Colony, 17
  education in, 15
  religion in, 14-15
  Salem witchcraft trials in, 15-16
Massachusetts 54th regiment, *30*
Massachusetts Institute of
      Technology (MIT), 44, 45
Massachusets (tribe), 8
Massachusetts Water Resources
      Authority (MWRA), 53
Massasoit, 14, 16, 60
Mather, Cotton, *16*
Mayflower, 12
medicine, 29, 44, 50
Merrimack River, 26, 52, *53*
Metacomet (King Philip), 16-17, 60
Minutemen, 20
Moody, Paul, 24
Morgan, William G., 35
Mott, Lucretia Coffin, 40
motto, state, 56

Naismith, James, 35
Nantucket, Massachusetts, 23, 46
Nashua River, 52, 53
Native Americans
  disease among, 8, 14
  explorers and, *11*
  in fur trade, 11
  in King Philip's War, 16, *17*
  settlers and, 14
  tribes, 8
  way of life, 8, *9*
Nausets, 8
Navigation Acts, 17
New Bedford, Massachusetts, 23, 42,
      43, 55
New Deal, 43
New England Antislavery Society, 28
New England Confederation, 16
New Hampshire, 15, 17
nickname, state, 56
Nipmucs, 8

Northampton, Massachusetts, 22

O'Brien, Hugh, 36
O'Neill, Thomas P. (Tip), *61*

Patuxets, 14
Pei, I. M., 46, 51
Pemaquids, 14
Pennacooks, 8
Pilgrims, *12*, *13*, 14
Plymouth Colony, *12*, *13*, 14, 16, 17
Pocomtucs, 8
police strike, 38
Poor, Salem, 21
population, 8, 14, 36, 55
power loom, 24, *26*
printing, *15*
prison reform, 34

Provincetown, Massachusetts, 12
Puritans, 13, 14-15, 32
  See also Massachusetts Bay Colony

Quakers, 14, *15*

radar, 44
religion
  Christian Science, 32, *33*
  of Pilgrims, 12, 13
  Puritan, 13, 14-15, 32
  transcendentalism, 32, *33*, 34
  Unitarians, 32, *33*
  Universalists, 32
Revere, Paul, 19, 20
Revolution, 40
Revolutionary War, 20, *21*, 22
Rhode Island, 15, 17
Roosevelt, Franklin D., 43

Sacco, Nicola, *41*, 42
Salem, Massachusetts
  China trade and, 23, *24-25*
  witchcraft trials in, 15-16
Samoset, 14
science, 34, *35*, 44, 45, 52
seal, state, *56*
shaman (medicine man), 8
Shawmut, 14
Shaw, Robert Gould, 30
Shay's Rebellion, *22*
shipbuilding, 23, 36
ships, *10*, 11, 17, 23, *24-25*, 36
shoe industry, 26
slavery, *27*
  abolitionists and, *27*, *28*, 29, 40
  Emancipation Proclamation, 30
  fugitive slaves, 28-29
socialism, 41
Sons of Liberty, 18, *20*, 21
sports, 35
Springfield, Massachusetts, *22*, 26,

      29, 35, *36*, 55
Squanto, 14, 60
Stamp Act, 18
Standish, John, 11
state government, 55
Stone, Lucy, 40, 60-61
strikes, 37-38, *39*
Sumner, Charles, *28*, 29

Tanglewood Music Festival, *45*
tar and feathers, *19*
taxes
  colonial, 18, *19*
  increase in, 48-49
Tea Act, 18
textile industry, 24, 26, 27, 37-38, *39*
Thanksgiving, 14
Thirteenth Amendment, 30
Thoreau, Henry David, 32, *33*, 34
tourism, *45*, 46
trade, 23, *24-25*
transcendentalism, 32, *33*, 34
Treaty of Ghent, 24
tree, state, *57*

Underground Railroad, 29
unemployment, 42-43, 49
Union Army, 29, *30*
Unitarians, 32, *33*
Universalists, 32

Vanzetti, Bartolomeo, *41*, 42
Verrazano, Giovanni da, 10
Vikings, *10*, 11
Vinland, 10

Walden (Thoreau), 34
Waltham, Massachusetts, 24
Wampanoags, 8, 9, 10, *11*, 14, 16, *17*
Wang, An, 61
War of 1812, 23-24
Washington, George, 22, 23
water pollution, 52-53
whaling, *7*, 23, 35
Wheatley, Phillis, *60*
White, Kevin H., 46
wigwams, 8, *9*
Winthrop, John, 14, 60
witchcraft, 15-16
Woman's Journal, 40
women
  in Civil War, *29*
  inequality of, 38
  in Salem witchcraft trials, 15-16
  suffrage movement and, 40
  in textile factories, 24, 26, 37-38, *39*
  in wartime industry, 44
Worcester, Massachusetts, 22, 26, 40,
      52, 55
World War II, 43-44